OUTHOUSES

IMAGES & CONTEMPLATIONS

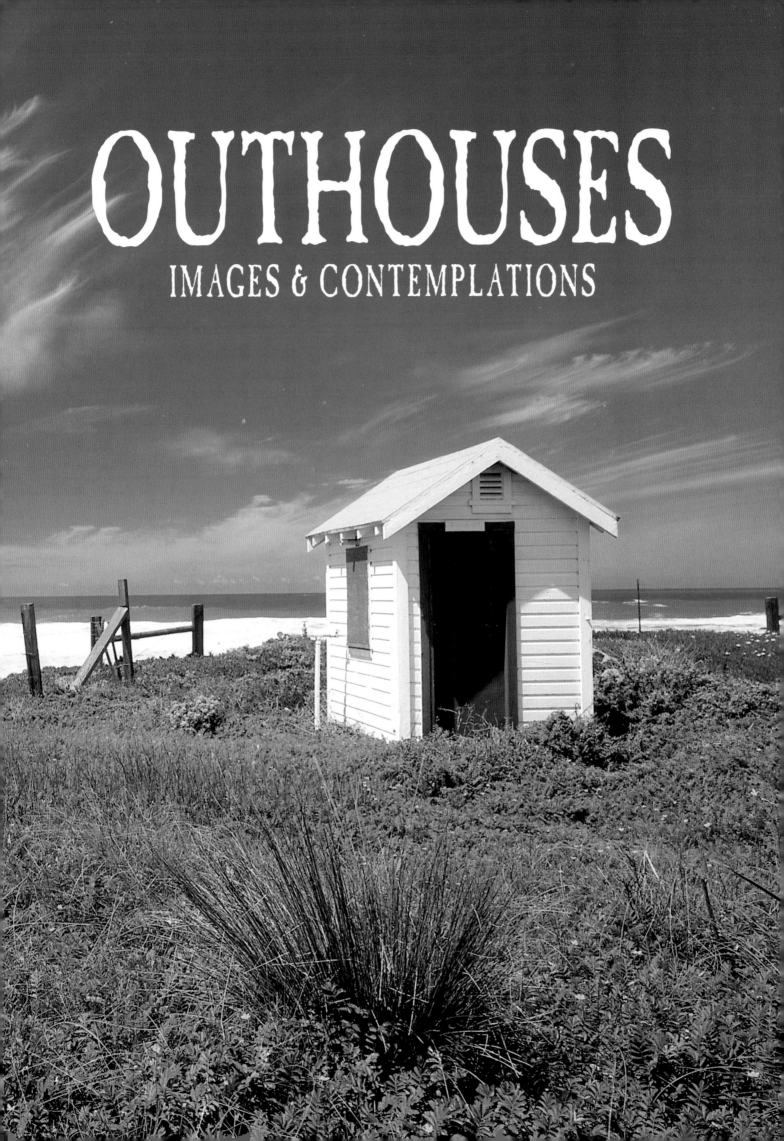

OUTHOUSES

IMAGES & CONTEMPLATIONS

Outhouse Photography Credits

Cover	©1998 Londie G. Padelsky	55	©1998 Jim Umhoefer
p. 2/3	©1998 Londie G. Padelsky	56/57	©1998 Londie G. Padelsky
5	©1998 Sherman Hines/Masterfile	58	©1998 Londie G. Padelsky
6/7	©1998 Londie G. Padelsky	59	©1998 Londie G. Padelsky
8	©1998 Londie G. Padelsky	60	©1998 Londie G. Padelsky
9	©1998 Londie G. Padelsky	61	©1998 Londie G. Padelsky
10	©1998 Londie G. Padelsky	62	©1998 Londie G. Padelsky
11	©1998 Londie G. Padelsky	63	©1998 Londie G. Padelsky
12	©1998 Londie G. Padelsky	64/65	©1998 Londie G. Padelsky
13	©1998 Londie G. Padelsky	66	©1998 Londie G. Padelsky
14	©1998 Londie G. Padelsky	67	©1998 Londie G. Padelsky
15	©1998 Fred Hirschmann	68	©1998 Londie G. Padelsky
16/17	©1998 Londie G. Padelsky	68	©1998 Howard A. Leistner
18/19	©1998 Londie G. Padelsky	69	©1998 Fred Hirschmann
20	©1998 Fred Hirschmann	70	©1998 Londie G. Padelsky
21	©1998 Fred Hirschmann	71	©1998 Howard A. Leistner
22	©1998 Londie G. Padelsky	72	©1998 Howard A. Leistner
22	©1998 Londie G. Padelsky	73	©1998 Carolyn Fox
23	©1998 Londie G. Padelsky	74	©1998 Jim Umhoefer
24/25	©1998 Londie G. Padelsky	75	©1998 Londie G. Padelsky
26	©1998 Fred Hirschmann	76	©1998 Londie G. Padelsky
27	©1998 Londie G. Padelsky	76	©1998 Londie G. Padelsky
27	©1998 Londie G. Padelsky	77	©1998 Carolyn Fox
28	©1998 Fred Hirschmann	78/79	©1998 Londie G. Padelsky
29	©1998 Londie G. Padelsky	80	©1998 Londie G. Padelsky
30	©1998 Larry Angier	81	©1998 Londie G. Padelsky
31	©1998 Paul Rezendes	82	©1998 Londie G. Padelsky
32	©1998 Londie G. Padelsky	83	©1998 Londie G. Padelsky
33	©1998 Londie G. Padelsky	84	©1998 Londie G. Padelsky
34/35	©1998 Londie G. Padelsky	85	©1998 Londie G. Padelsky
36	©1998 Londie G. Padelsky	86/87	©1998 Londie G. Padelsky
37	©1998 Londie G. Padelsky	88/89	©1998 Londie G. Padelsky
37	©1998 Londie G. Padelsky	90	©1998 Fred Hirschmann
38	©1998 Londie G. Padelsky	91	©1998 Londie G. Padelsky
38	©1998 Londie G. Padelsky	92	©1998 Londie G. Padelsky
39	©1998 Londie G. Padelsky	93	©1998 MS Neidig
40	©1998 Londie G. Padelsky	94	©1998 Londie G. Padelsky
41	©1998 Londie G. Padelsky	95	©1998 Londie G. Padelsky
42/43	©1998 Fred Hirschmann	96/97	©1998 Larry Turner
44	©1998 Fred Hirschmann	98/99	©1998 Londie G. Padelsky
45	©1998 Londie G. Padelsky	100	©1998 Londie G. Padelsky
46/47	©1998 Londie G. Padelsky	101	©1998 Fred Hirschmann
48/49	©1998 Londie G. Padelsky	102/103	©1998 Londie G. Padelsky
50/51	©1998 Londie G. Padelsky	104/105	©1998 Londie G. Padelsky
52	©1998 Londie G. Padelsky	106	©1998 Sherman Hines/Masterfile
53	©1998 Londie G. Padelsky	107	©1998 Sherman Hines/Masterfile
53	©1998 Londie G. Padelsky	108/109	©1998 Sherman Hines/Masterfile
54	©1998 Londie G. Padelsky	110/111	©1998 Sherman Hines/Masterfile

Entire Contents
©1998 BrownTrout Publishers, Inc.
Photography ©1998 The respective photographers

Library of Congress Cataloging-in-Publication Data
Outhouses : images & contemplations.
        p.   cm.
      ISBN 1-56313-927-8 (alk. paper)
      1. Outhouses–Pictorial works.   I. BrownTrout Publishers.
TD775.088   1998
392.3'6–dc21
                                                98-39588
                                                CIP

Printed and bound in Italy by Milanostampa

ISBN: 1-56313-927-8 (alk. paper)
10 9 8 7 6 5 4 3 2 1
Digit on the right indicates the number of this printing

Published by:
BrownTrout Publishers, Inc.
Post Office Box 280070
San Francisco, California 94128-0070 U.S.A.

Toll Free: 800 777 7812
Website: browntrout.com

"Out upon it, I have loved
  Three whole days together!
And am like to love three more;
  If it prove fair weather."
                    — *John Suckling*

"As nature of any given thing is the aggregate of its powers and properties, so nature in the abstract is the aggregate of the powers and properties of all things. Nature means the sum of all phenomena together with the causes which produce them; including not only all that happens, but all that is capable of happening."

— *John Stuart Mill*

Every great man is always being helped by everybody, for his gift is to get good out of all things and all persons."

— *John Ruskin*

"If you want to be happy, be."
— *Alexei Konstantinovich Tolstoi*

"Conduct your blooming in the noise and whip
of the whirlwind."
— *Gwendolyn Brooks*

"Afoot and light-hearted I take to
the open road,
Healthy, free, the world before me,
The long brown path before me
leading
Wherever I choose."

— *Walt Whitman*

"I will make you brooches and
toys for your delight
Of birdsong at morning and
starshine at night."
— *Robert Louis Stevenson*

"My dear, I don't care what they do,
so long as they don't do it in the
street and frighten the horses."
— *Mrs. Patrick Campbell*

"No house should ever be *on* any hill or on anything.
It should be *of* the hill, belonging to it, so hill and house
could live together each the happier for the other."

— *Frank Lloyd Wright*

"Little friend of all the world."
— *Rudyard Kipling*

"Dream, dream, for this is also sooth."
— *William Butler Yeats*

"I have come home to look after my fences."
— *John Sherman*

"Man, if you gotta ask you'll never know."
— *Louis Armstrong*

"Dreams are necessary to life."

— *Anaïs Nin*

"What nature delivers to us is never stale.
Because what nature creates has eternity in it.'

— *Isaac Bashevis Singer*

"The greatness of art is not to find what is common but what is unique."

— *Isaac Bashevis Singer*

"Turn up the lights — I don't want to go home in the dark."

— *Last words of O. Henry*

"If you don't say anything, you
won't be called on to repeat it."
— *Calvin Coolidge*

41

"The clearest way into the universe is through a forest wilderness."

— *John Muir*

"Ah, madman! Whom are you
running away from?
Gods too have lived in the woods."
— *Virgil*

"All nature wears one universal grin."

— *Henry Fielding*

"I went to the woods because I wished to live deliberately,
to front only the essential facts of life, and see if I could not
learn what it had to teach, and not, when I came to die
discover that I had not lived."
— *Henry David Thoreau*

"Time is but the stream I go a-fishing in."
— *Henry David Thoreau*

"The one who goes is happier
Than those he leaves behind."
— *Edward Pollock*

"Art is the right hand of nature.
The latter has only given us being;
the former has made us men."
— *J.C.F. Schiller*

"Beautiful as sweet!
And young as beautiful!
And soft as young!
And gay as soft!
And innocent as gay!"
— *Edward Young*

57

"A full belly doth not engender a subtle wit."

— *George Pettie*

"Tout est pour le meiux dans le meilleur des mondes possibles"

— *Volta*

"Thou shalt make castles then in Spain,
And dream of joy, all but in vain."
— *Geoffrey Chaucer*

"When all candles be out, all cats be grey."
— *John Heywood*

61

"Character is higher than intellect.
Thinking is the function.
Living is the functionary."
— *Ralph Waldo Emerson*

"Tomorrow to fresh woods, and pastures new."
— *John Milton*

"Coffee should be black as Hell,
strong as death, and sweet as love."
— *Turkish proverb*

"There is no love sincerer than the love of food."

— *George Bernard Shaw*

"The purest and most thoughtful minds are those which love color the most."

— *John Ruskin*

"Friendship, of itself a holy tie,
Is made more sacred by adversity."

— *John Dryden*

"Every natural action is graceful."

— *Ralph Waldo Emerson*

"No one can give you better advice than yourself."

— *Cicero*

"The day becomes more solemn and serene
When noon is past."

— *Percy Bysshe Shelle*

"By all means, use sometimes to be alone;
Salute thyself; see what thy soul doth wear."

— *George Herbert*

"Allegory lives in a transparent palace."

— *A.M. Lemierre*

"Action is only coarsened thought — thought
 become concrete, obscure, and unconscious."

— *H.F. Amiel*

"Never take the antidote before the poison."
("Ne prius antidotum quam venenum.")

— *Latin proverb*

"Action may not always bring happiness; but there is no happiness without action."

— *Benjamin Disraeli*

"He who lays a good egg has a
right to cackle."

— *Proverb*

"Does the road wind uphill all the way?
Yes, to the very end.
Will the day's journey take the whole long day?
From morn to night, my friend."

— *Christina Georgina Rossetti*

"To know is nothing at all; to imagine is everything."

— *Anatole France*

"And pluck till time and times are done
The silver apples of the moon,
The golden apples of the sun."
— *William Butler Yeats*

"Now I adore my life
With the Bird, the abiding Leaf,
With the Fish, the questing Snail,
And the Eye altering all;
And I dance with William Blake
For love, for Love's sake."
— *Theodore Roethke*

"A musician must make music, an artist must paint,
  a poet must write, if he is to be ultimately at peace with himself.
  What a man can be, he must be."
                                        — *Abraham Harold Maslow*

"Well, this is the end of a perfect day,
  Near the end of a journey, too.
                              — *Carrie Jacobs Bond*

"It is not raining rain to me,
    It's raining daffodils.
It is not raining rain to me,
    It's raining violets."
                — *Robert Loveman*

"A great nose indicates a great man —
Genial, courteous, intellectual,
Virile, courageous."
— *Edmond Rostand*

"Look homeward, angel."

— *John Milton*

"Learn from the birds what food the thickets yield;
Learn from the beasts the physic of the field;
The arts of building from the bee receive;
Learn of the mole to plow, the worm to weave."

— *Alexander Pope*

"Man is a two-legged animal without feathers."

— *Plato*

"Patience and time accomplish more than force and violence."

— *La Fontaine*

"Like a postage stamp, a man's value depends on his ability to stick to a thing till he gets there."

— *Joseph Chamberlain*

"The future belongs to him who knows how to wait."

— *Russian proverb*

"Philosophy teaches a knowledge
of the truth of things."
— *Hegel*

"Never yet was a springtime
When the buds forgot to blow."
— *Margaret Elizabeth Sangster*

"When Nature has work to be done, she creates a genius to do it."

— *Ralph Waldo Emerson*

'If with me you'd fondly stray,
 Over the hills and far way."

— *John Gay*

"We think our fathers fools,
so wise we grow;
Our wiser sons, no doubt,
will think us so."

— *Alexander Pope*

103

"Always leave something to wish for, otherwise you will be miserable from your very happiness."

— *Baltasar Gracián*

"The longer the path, the sweeter the way home."

— *Proverb*

"Night brings out the stars."

— *Proverb*

"There's no head like an old head."
— *Proverb*

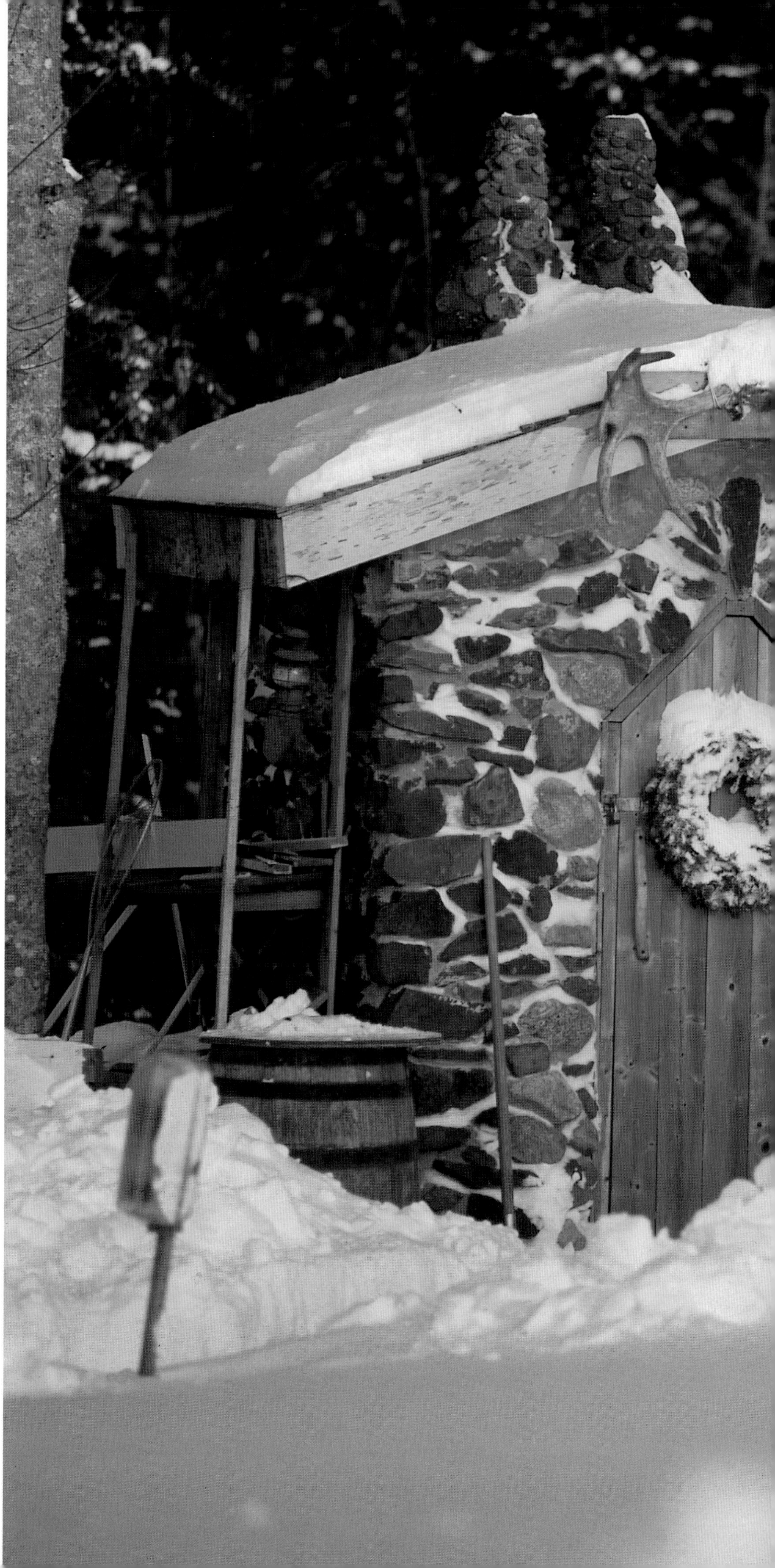

"The moon like a flower
    In heaven's high tower,
    With silent delight,
    Sits and smiles on the night."
            — *William Blake*

111